VOL. 60

HAL•LEONARD®

VIOLIN PLAY-ALONG

AUDIO ACCESS INCLUDED

PLAYBACK+
Speed • Pitch • Balance • Loop

THE BEATLES

T0088781

CONTENTS

To access online content visit:
www.halleonard.com/mylibrary

7591-0422-1855-4766

ISBN 978-1-4950-5621-5

HAL•LEONARD®
CORPORATION

7777 W. BLUEMOUND RD. P.O. BOX 13819 MILWAUKEE, WI 53213

Jon Vriesacker, violin
Audio arrangements by Peter Deneff
Recorded and Produced by Jake Johnson
at Paradyme Productions

All You Need Is Love

Words and Music by John Lennon and Paul McCartney

D.S. al Coda

CODA

3

Blackbird

Words and Music by John Lennon and Paul McCartney

Hey Jude

Words and Music by John Lennon and Paul McCartney

Let It Be

Words and Music by John Lennon and Paul McCartney

Love Me Do
Words and Music by John Lennon and Paul McCartney

Ob-La-Di, Ob-La-Da

Words and Music by John Lennon and Paul McCartney

With a Little Help from My Friends

Words and Music by John Lennon and Paul McCartney

Yesterday

Words and Music by John Lennon and Paul McCartney